Latin American
and
Caribbean Crafts

Latin American
and
Caribbean Crafts

Judith Hoffman Corwin

FRANKLIN WATTS
New York/London/Toronto/Sydney

Also by Judith Hoffman Corwin

AFRICAN CRAFTS
ASIAN CRAFTS
COLONIAL AMERICAN CRAFTS: THE HOME
COLONIAL AMERICAN CRAFTS: THE SCHOOL
COLONIAL AMERICAN CRAFTS: THE VILLAGE
PAPERCRAFTS

For Jules Arthur and Oliver Jamie

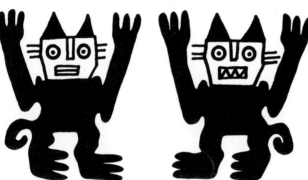

Library of Congress Cataloging-in-Publication Data

Corwin, Judith Hoffman.
    Latin American and Caribbean crafts / Judith Hoffman Corwin
      p.   cm.
    Includes index.
    Summary: A potpourri of recipes and craft and folklore projects
from Latin America and the Caribbean.
    ISBN 0-531-11014-1
    1. Handicraft—Latin America—Juvenile literature.   2. Handicraft—
Caribbean Area—Juvenile literature.   3. Cookery, Latin American—
Juvenile literature. 4. Cookery, Caribbean—Juvenile literature.
[1. Handicraft—Latin America.   2. Handicraft—Caribbean Area.
3. Cookery, Latin American.   4. Cookery, Caribbean.] I. Title.
TT27.5.C67   1991
745.5—dc20   91-13466
                                  CIP
                                  AC

Contents

Introduction

The people of Latin America and the Caribbean have made great contributions to the culture of the world in the field of the arts. Before the arrival of Columbus in America, the ancient civilizations of this area of the world created masterpieces in gold and silver. Today all of this ancient history and culture is being looked at again and appreciated for its great artistic value.

In this book, you will learn how to make things in the style of both the ancient and modern Latin American and Caribbean cultures, using materials that can mostly be found in your home. The Indians of ancient Latin America made masks and idols out of gold and silver and sculptures out of clay; they wove intricate textiles and painted lovely scenes with pictures of people and animals on them.

Through art, young people can learn something about the history and customs of this part of the world. Art enriches both our understanding of and respect for other peoples and cultures. Through projects inspired by Latin American and Caribbean objects, crafts, and food, ordinary everyday materials can be messengers of these faraway places.

The crafts of both ancient and modern Latin America and the Caribbean are important because they have produced functional, decorative, and expressive objects. Craft techniques were passed on from father to son and mother to daughter so that they would remain alive. Today they are a true link to a cultural past and heritage.

This book is filled with ideas, information, folklore, and recipes. They help to show that crafts know no boundaries—they are a basic human artistic expression. After all, there is only one world.

By following the clear and simple instructions included, you will be able to make many nice things. Explore and appreciate how Latin American and Caribbean artists create designs in their own special way to capture the unique spirit of their cultures. You will also want to experiment and create your very own projects.

Traditional Latin American and Caribbean Designs ◆◆

On the next few pages, you will find an exciting selection of traditional Latin American and Caribbean designs. There are simple, abstract, and geometric ones. There are designs of people and flowers, especially the Spanish rose, Mexican sunflower, and Caribbean hibiscus. There are also animal designs to choose from—the hummingbird, starfish, shark, sea horse, anteater, llama, alpaca, and armadillo. They can all be used on stationery, greeting cards, wrapping paper, pictures, and T-shirts. Just use your imagination. These interesting designs can serve as inspiration for your own original drawings. You can have fun drawing them larger or smaller, and changing them as you like. To begin, all you need is a pencil and a piece of paper.

Monster Molas

The women of Panama have invented a clever method of applying one piece of fabric to another, or appliquéing. It is called molas, and it is a cut-through type of appliqué. The design is created by cutting through layers of fine-colored cotton fabric, exposing the various colors underneath it. The edges of the shapes are turned under and then sewn together with tiny stitches.

This appliquéd fabric was originally used to make clothing, but it is so special that everyone wanted a sample to hang on the wall as a decoration. We will be making a molas in the design of a monster. It will be done in a simplified way: gluing colored felt and fabric together. Four layers will be used to create a design that is commanding because of the strong use of combined color.

HERE'S WHAT YOU WILL NEED:

7″ × 9″ piece of white fabric, for the background
7″ × 9″ piece of black felt, for top first layer
pencil, tracing paper
scissors, straight pins, glue
scraps of felt in white, yellow, pink, red, orange, green, blue, and black
    for monster's stripes and features

HERE'S HOW TO DO IT:

1. Place the white background fabric on your working surface, smoothing it out nicely. You are going to be putting layers of other fabric on top of this to make your monster molas.

2. With the pencil, trace the pattern for the black felt onto the tracing paper. Pin the tracing paper to the piece of black felt. Cut it out. Remove the pins and tracing paper.

3. Carefully place the black felt on top of the white background fabric. Glue in place.

4. Cut strips from the colored felt, as shown in the illustration. Glue in place.

14

5. To make the monster's eyes, cut two circles from the white felt and then cut two smaller circles from the black felt, checking the illustration for proper size. First, glue the white circles onto the face. Then glue the black circles on top of the white ones.

6. Checking the illustration, cut out a tongue from the red felt, a nose from the green felt, and whiskers from the orange felt. Glue all of these pieces in place.

16

Caribbean Village Scene ◆ ◆ ◆

This folk-art village scene is symbolic of the ones found in Cuba, Guatemala, and the Dominican Republic. Here's another chance to let your imagination run wild. You can make the simple, bold houses, trees, and animals as colorful as you like. The black background will give this a very dramatic effect. Fill up the whole scene with as much as you can. Check the illustration for ideas—make a moon and lots of stars in the sky, rows of trees, with houses in between, and small groups of animals. In the bottom right-hand corner, make a pond and some ducks to swim in it.

HERE'S WHAT YOU WILL NEED:

1 sheet of black oaktag
1 sheet of blue oaktag
scraps of colored felt—yellow, orange, red, pink, blue, green, brown, and gray
scraps of brightly colored fabric with a small print
2 sheets of 11″ × 14″ tracing paper
pencil, scissors
straight pins, glue stick

HERE'S HOW TO DO IT:

1. Designs for a tree, house, chicken, duck, goat, moon, and stars are shown. With a pencil, trace the designs onto the tracing paper. These will be your patterns. Cut them out and pin the patterns onto the fabric that you choose to work with. Cut out the fabric. Remove the tracing paper patterns. The patterns can be used over and over again. Fill up the whole piece of oaktag. You can start by making a blue sky and a row of trees, as shown. Fill in the spaces with several houses and then scatter the animals around. Put the pond with the ducks in the bottom corner.

2. When you have completed your village scene and have filled it up with lots of colored felt and printed cotton fabric designs, you are ready to glue them to the background. Take the glue stick and spread an even amount of glue on the back of each piece of fabric. Now put the piece back where it came from. Start doing this at the top, with the sky and trees, and work your way down. Enjoy your finished picture and display it proudly. ◆ ◆ ◆ ◆ ◆ ◆ ◆ ◆ ◆ ◆

Blustery Blackbeard

The Caribbean was visited by Christopher Columbus in 1493. Spain claimed the area, and its ships searched for treasure. The Caribbean Sea became a main route for Spanish ships carrying the treasures of the New World to the mother country. These large, slow-moving vessels were easy prey for the enemies of Spain, who gave permission to pirates (privateers) to attack Spanish ships in the Caribbean and take their precious cargo. Soon, many pirates began to operate on their own. These reckless outlaws were called buccaneers, and they used the many islands of the Caribbean as places to rest and to hide their treasure.

Blackbeard was a striking, fierce, legendary pirate. He and his crew raided ships, looting their treasures. His ship flew the Jolly Roger—the dreaded black pirate flag with the white skull and crossbones in the middle. He was called Blackbeard because of his long, black, bushy beard and hair. Blackbeard wore a sling over his shoulder with three pistols hanging in holsters. His eyes had a strange, wild look about them. He wanted to scare his sailors and keep them loyal and obedient.

We will be making a Blackbeard jumping jack out of oaktag. He can move his arms and legs, and he is carrying a Jolly Roger flag.

HERE'S WHAT YOU WILL NEED:

No. 2 soft lead pencil, tracing paper
teaspoon
white oaktag
black fine-line felt-tip marker, scissors
hole punch
8 brass paper fasteners
2 4" pieces of string
12" piece of string
small bead (its hole must be large enough for the string to go through)
scrap of black fabric, toothpick, glue

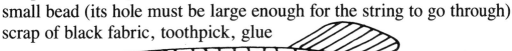

HERE'S HOW TO DO IT:

1. Use the pencil to trace the patterns onto the tracing paper.

2. Place the pencil-marked side of the tracing paper on top of the oaktag. Use the teaspoon to rub firmly along the pencil lines until all of the patterns are transferred onto the oaktag.

3. Draw over all of these lines with the black fine-line felt-tip marker. Color in the black areas, checking the illustration. Cut out the pieces.

4. With the hole punch, make the holes in the body, arm, and leg pieces where indicated by black dots on the patterns.

5. Attach boots to the legs with brass fasteners. Fasten arm sections together. Using hole A in arms and hole B in legs, attach them to the body, as shown in the illustration. Place arms and legs in back of the body.

6. Turn the body so that the back is facing you. Place it flat on your working surface. With a 4″ piece of string, connect top holes in arms. Be sure to knot the string securely, as shown. Take the other 4″ piece of string and connect the legs. Using the third piece of string (the 12″ one), tie one end to the center of the string connecting the arms. Then take the string down and tie it to the center of the string connecting the legs. Do this very gently, being careful not to pull the string too tight. Now tie a bead on the end of the string.

7. To move the arms and legs up and down, hold Blackbeard's hat with one hand and pull the bead end of the string downward with the other.

8. Checking the illustration, cut the flag out of the scrap of black fabric. Take a scrap of the white oaktag and draw the skeleton head and daggers. Cut them out and glue them to the black fabric. Attach the flag to the top half of the toothpick and glue it to Blackbeard's hand, as shown in the illustration.

Sculpturing Dough ◆◆◆◆◆

This is a homemade sculpting dough that can be made easily and will harden to dry naturally. It's fun to experiment with—just roll it out, cut it up into fancy designs, or shape it with your hands. You can try making it into some of the traditional designs shown on pages 8–11. They can be painted in bright and crazy colors. The dough is also used to make the Pre-Columbian king figure, Peruvian scary cat, and ancient Inca idol.

HERE'S WHAT YOU WILL NEED:

Ingredients

2 cups baking soda
1 cup cornstarch
1¼ cups water

Utensils

measuring cups
medium saucepan, mixing spoon
dinner plate, two paper towels
cookie sheet

HERE'S HOW TO DO IT: ◆◆◆◆◆◆

1. Put all three ingredients into the saucepan and stir until completely combined. Put the saucepan on the stove. Ask an adult to help you turn on the stove. Heat the mixture until it thickens to modeling consistency. This should take about 5 minutes on a medium-high light on the stove.

2. Take the saucepan off the stove. Remove the dough and put it on the dinner plate. Wet the paper towels and put them over the dough. Allow the dough to cool. Now it is ready to be rolled, shaped, or cut into whatever you want to make out of it.

The great thing about this kind of sculpting dough is that it will harden in a day or two all by itself. If you want it to harden faster, you can bake it in the oven.

3. To bake it in the oven, first ask an adult to turn the oven on to 350°. Preheat the oven for 15 minutes and then turn it off. Put your finished piece of sculpture on a cookie sheet and ask an adult to put it into the oven for you. Leave it in the oven for half an hour.

4. Remove the baked, cooled piece from the oven and paint it with acrylic paints.

Pre-Columbian King Figure

One of the best ways to learn about how people lived or what was important to them is to look at and study their artwork. Their buildings, stone-paved roads, household objects, sculptures, textiles, gold and silver ornaments, jewelry and pottery can all give you some idea of what people's lives were like long ago.

You can make a little sculpture just like the ones made in Latin America five hundred to a thousand years ago. Paint the object brown, and it will look very much like the magical figures found in museums today.

HERE'S WHAT YOU WILL NEED:

1½ cups dough (follow recipe on page 24)
pencil, brown acrylic paint, paintbrush

HERE'S HOW TO DO IT:

1. This Pre-Columbian king figure is really quite expressive, even though he stands only about 8″ high, including his crown. He is made out of the dough that is described on page 24. You will use the dough to make the different parts of his body. Then you'll put them together to form your figure.

2. Begin by making: 1 2″ ball, for the head
2 1½″ × 5″ rolls, for the body and legs; 1 roll, 8″ long, for the arms

3. Join the two rolls that are for the body and legs from the top to about 2″ down, pinching together the dough and smoothing it out as you work. This top part will become the body. Bend out the bottom of each roll slightly, as shown in the illustration, to form the feet. Push the legs down as you are working, so that the figure will stand up.

4. Attach the head, again pushing it into the body and pinching the dough together. Then smooth it out and make a little neck.

5. To make the face, first check the illustration that shows the side view. This will give you an idea of how to shape the nose. Start by taking some dough, about the size of a penny, and shaping it like a cone. Press it into place and shape it until it is smooth and looks like the illustration.

6. Now make two small balls for eyes and attach them to the face. Press the point of the pencil into the center of each eye to make an eyeball. Take bits of dough and make eyebrows, ears, and a mouth, as shown, and attach them, smoothing and shaping as needed.

7. For the crown, make a ¼″ roll of clay that will fit around the head and attach it. Make the crown points and three small balls, and attach them. Press them into place on the crown, as shown.

8. Leave the figure out to dry for a day or two, or bake it in an oven, as described on page 24. Cover the figure with the brown acrylic paint and allow to dry. Now it is ready to display and enjoy.

Ancient Peruvian Idol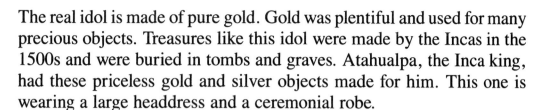

The real idol is made of pure gold. Gold was plentiful and used for many precious objects. Treasures like this idol were made by the Incas in the 1500s and were buried in tombs and graves. Atahualpa, the Inca king, had these priceless gold and silver objects made for him. This one is wearing a large headdress and a ceremonial robe.

HERE'S WHAT YOU WILL NEED:

1½ cups dough (follow recipe on page 24)
rolling pin, waxed paper
pencil, tracing paper, scissors
knife
gold paint, brush
black fine-line felt-tip marker

HERE'S HOW TO DO IT:

1. Take the dough and roll it out to ¼″ thickness on a sheet of waxed paper. It should make about a 7″ square.

2. Trace the drawing onto the tracing paper with the pencil and then cut it out. Put the tracing paper onto the rolled-out dough.

3. Using the knife carefully, cut all around the outside edge.

4. Checking the illustration on the previous page, carve into the dough with the point of the pencil to make the eyes, nose, mouth, and the inside of the ears. Also carve the designs on the headdress and robe. Press hard enough so that the impression will remain after the dough hardens.

5. Allow the dough to dry naturally, or bake it according to the directions on page 24.

6. Cover the idol with the gold paint. First paint one side and then the other. With the black fine-line felt-tip marker, go over some of the details of the idol. You can draw over his face and some of the designs on his headdress and robe.

Scary Black Cats

This scary black cat design is taken from a Peruvian textile that was created by the Inca Indians in the 1500s. Some of the most exciting textiles in the world were made by these spinners and weavers. The colorful yarn used was spun by hand, from cotton and wool that came from alpacas and llamas.

This historic feline, with two rows of teeth, is scary enough to delight us more than four hundred years later. We are going to be making two versions of the cat—a large cat that can be taped to a window and a smaller one that is a pin and can be worn on a T-shirt.

Large Scary Black Cat

This large cat is made of black oaktag and is great to tape onto a window.

HERE'S WHAT YOU WILL NEED:

pencil, tracing paper
black oaktag, scissors
white paper
glue, tape

HERE'S HOW TO DO IT:

1. With the pencil, trace the large cat drawing on the next page onto the tracing paper. Cut it out. Put the tracing paper on top of the black oaktag. Hold this in one hand, and, with the other hand, cut along the pencil line.

2. Cut out two eyes and teeth from the white paper, as shown in the illustration. Glue in place on the cat's face. Tape your scary black cat to a window and watch everyone stare at it.

Scary Black Cat Pin

HERE'S WHAT YOU WILL NEED:

¼ cup of sculpturing dough
rolling pin, waxed paper
pencil, tracing paper, scissors
knife
black and white acrylic paints
paintbrush
safety pin, glue

HERE'S HOW TO DO IT:

1. Follow the directions given on page 24 for making the sculpturing dough.

2. On a sheet of waxed paper, roll out ¼ cup of dough to a ¼″ thickness.

3. With the pencil, trace the smaller drawing of the cat onto the tracing paper. Cut it out. Now put the drawing on the rolled-out dough.

4. Cut all around the outside edge of the dough with the knife. Allow the dough to dry naturally, or bake following the directions given on page 24.

5. Paint the cat all black, and then let it dry. Now, checking the illustration, paint the eyes and teeth with the white paint. Glue the safety pin to the reverse side of the cat. Now your pin is ready to wear!

Mexican Bark Paintings

Bright, bold bark paintings are made mostly in Mexico, but similar ones can be found in Puerto Rico and Brazil. These beautiful paintings are actually painted right on the bark of a tree. The bark is peeled off and smoothed down. Usually pictures of birds, trees, and flowers are painted on the bark using bright colors, leaving the unpainted bark as the background.

We will be making a painting on a piece of plywood, which is like the bark that the native artists painted on. Get a scrap of plywood from your local lumberyard if you don't have any at home. Designs are given for some birds, flowers, and two rabbits.

HERE'S WHAT YOU WILL NEED:

tracing paper, carbon paper
tape, pencil
$1/4''$ thick scrap of plywood, about $8'' \times 10''$ (one piece is needed for each of the designs)
permanent black fine-line felt-tip marker
acrylic paints in yellow, orange, red, pink, blue, and green
paintbrushes
shellac and paintbrush, optional

HERE'S HOW TO DO IT:

1. Choose which design you would like to make on your plywood. Use the pencil to trace the design onto the tracing paper.

2. Place the carbon paper on the scrap of plywood. Tape it on the top and bottom to hold it down. Put the tracing paper design on top of the carbon paper and tape it down. With the pencil, go over the design, pressing hard as you draw.

3. Remove the tracing paper and carbon paper. Now go over the lines on the plywood with the permanent black fine-line felt-tip marker.

4. Color in the drawing—only the designs—with the acrylic paints. Don't be afraid to use your imagination when you work. Just remember that the drawing should be lively and bright. Leave the background wood showing.

5. When you have finished coloring your painting, you may want to put a coat of shellac over it. This will seal the painting and give it a glossy look.

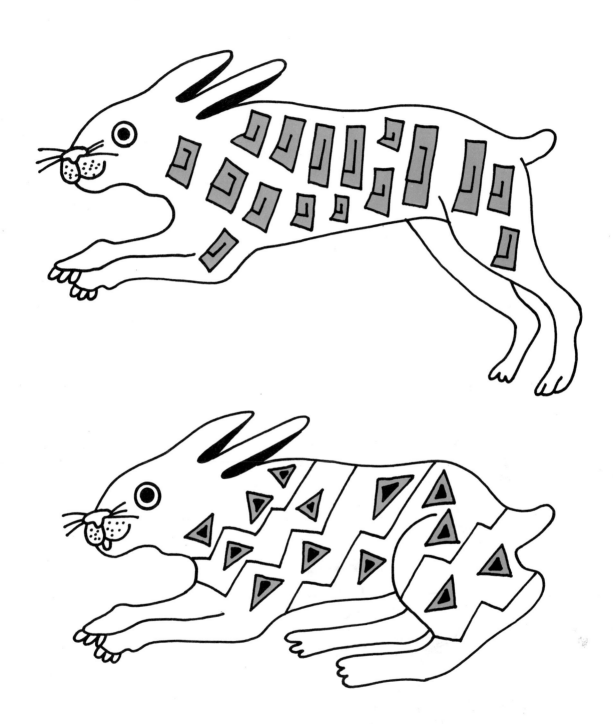

Wild Watercolors of the Tropics ◆◆◆◆◆◆◆◆◆◆◆◆

These creatures of the tropics are wildly colorful—sparkling yellows, reds, turquoises, oranges, and greens cover them.

The toucan is a brightly colored bird that is at home in the Brazilian jungle, where it can happily eat the plentiful fruit and insects. The toucan has large black eyes and an enormous lime green, orange, lemon yellow, flame red, and sea-breeze turquoise beak.

The Mexican angelfish swims freely in the tropical waters along the coral reefs off the coast of Mexico. Colored in turquoise, yellow, and green, this fish seems unreal because of its gorgeous coloring. It's almost as if an artist brought out a box of paints and created these truly magnificent creatures.

These two wild and wonderful creatures can be painted in watercolors and enjoyed as a brilliant, colorful reflection of Latin America.

HERE'S WHAT YOU WILL NEED:

3 pieces of 8″ × 10″ watercolor paper (1 sheet is to be used for experimenting)
small box of watercolors—yellow, red, orange, blue, green, and black
paintbrushes
tracing paper
pencil, carbon paper
permanent fine-line felt-tip marker
container for clean water
container for water to clean the brushes in
paper towel to dry off brushes

HERE'S HOW TO DO IT:

1. Before beginning to make your pictures, you can have fun experimenting with mixing up some special colors with the watercolors. Try making lime green—mix yellow with a little blue. To make turquoise, mix blue with a little green; and to make flame red, mix red with a little yellow.

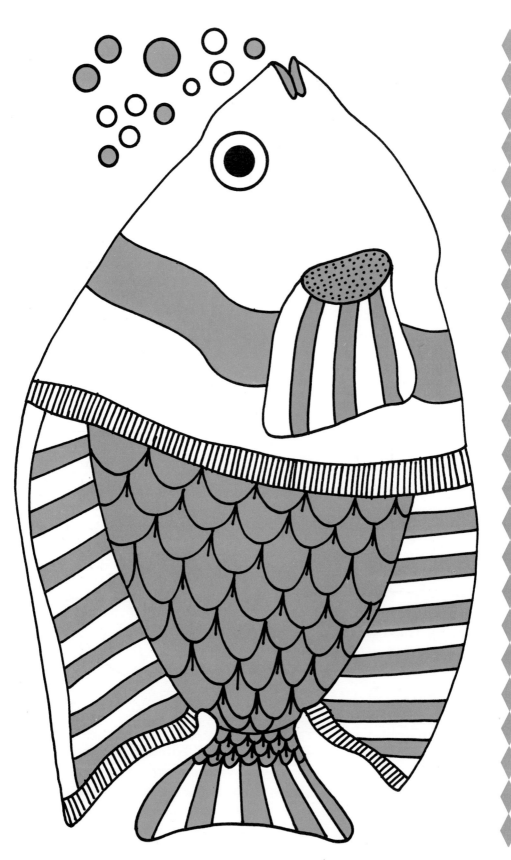

2. Now try experimenting with the watercolor paper. First put the brush into the clean water and spread it across the paper. Now put a dot of paint onto the water and watch it spread. It makes a nice design and will give your painting an interesting look. Allow the paper to dry, without moving it. Also try spreading some paint on the paper and then touching it with another color. The two colors will mix where they touch, and a third color will be made. You can also just spread some watercolor on the dry paper. Try using different amounts of water on the brush, and you will get varying colors. Some will be brighter than others—the less water you use, the stronger the color will come out.

3. With the pencil, trace the designs on the tracing paper. Place the carbon paper on the watercolor paper and then put your tracing over it. Go over all the pencil lines on the tracing paper again. Remove the tracing and carbon papers. Now go over all the lines with the black fine-line felt-tip marker. Do this for both pictures.

4. Using the colors that you like and following the illustrations, use the watercolors and techniques to complete your paintings.

Tropical Island Collage ◆◆◆

The Caribbean islands are magical places—clear, blue skies, warm water, pink sandy beaches, tall royal palm trees, golden sun, cool sea breezes blowing a tiny white sailboat. Who could resist such an idyllic scene?

We will be making this dreamy scene, using colored tissue paper and gluing it onto a background with polymer medium, which is spread on with your fingers. The color of the tissue paper "bleeds" slightly when the polymer medium is spread on. It gives the scene a nice "watery" feeling. You can also use regular colored paper and glue it onto the background. You could even draw the scene with felt-tip markers or colored pencils, or do it in watercolors.

HERE'S WHAT YOU WILL NEED:

7″ × 10″ piece of white oaktag (there will be a 1″ border around the picture)
colored tissue paper in light blue, dark blue, light green, dark green, pink, red, and yellow
polymer medium (you can get this in an art supply store)
pencil, tracing paper, scissors
black fine-line felt-tip marker
glue, white paper
red colored pencil

HERE'S HOW TO DO IT:

1. Checking the illustrations, you will see that this scene is made up of strips of colored tissue paper. Cut two light blue strips, one for the water and one for the sky. Cut one dark blue strip for the sky. Cut one in pink for the sand and one in light green for the grass.

2. Arrange the strips on the oaktag, as shown in the illustration. Beginning with the pieces for the sky, spread enough polymer medium over each strip to keep it in place. It should completely cover the strip. Smooth out the tissue paper as you work. Repeat for all five strips. Allow them to dry thoroughly, about an hour.

3. With the pencil, draw the palm tree on the tracing paper. The palm tree is in two colors of green tissue paper. Cut the palm tree into two parts, the top leaves and the trunk. Now hold the tracing paper on the tissue paper and cut it out. The leaves are cut from the light green tissue paper. The trunk gets cut from the dark green tissue paper. Using the polymer medium and checking the illustration for proper placement, glue the tree onto the scene.

4. Cut a circle for the sun out of the yellow tissue paper and spread polymer medium over it to secure it.

5. To make the sailboat, check the illustration and sketch it onto the scene with the pencil. Now go over the lines with the black fine-line felt-tip marker. Cut out the boat and the sail from the white paper. Put a little glue on the back of them and press them into the scene. With the red colored pencil make two stripes on the sail.

Mexican Cocoa Balls

The people of Mexico have enjoyed chocolate for centuries, well before it was brought to the United States. These tiny cocoa balls taste super and don't even have to be baked. They can be made in a flash and stored in an airtight tin.

HERE'S WHAT YOU WILL NEED:

Ingredients

1 cup sugar
4 tablespoons orange juice
1 cup finely chopped nuts
$\frac{1}{2}$ cup finely chopped candied fruits
$\frac{1}{2}$ cup unsweetened cocoa powder

Utensils

measuring cups and spoons
saucepan, mixing spoon
waxed paper
pot holder

HERE'S HOW TO DO IT:

1. Ask an adult to help you turn on the stove and watch you do the cooking. In the saucepan, over medium-high heat, combine the sugar and orange juice. Stir until combined and the sugar dissolves.

2. Remove the pan from the stove and allow the mixture to cool. Add the chopped nuts and candied fruit.

3. With clean hands, shape the dough into balls, about the size of large marbles. Sprinkle the cocoa powder onto the waxed paper and then roll the balls in it until they are completely coated. Share some cocoa balls with friends and store the leftovers in a tin. Makes about two dozen balls.

Bunuelos—Colombian Sweet Fritters

These yummy little treats are traditionally prepared for special occasions, like Christmas Eve. We can make them anytime and enjoy their sweet taste and smell.

HERE'S WHAT YOU WILL NEED:

Ingredients

3 tablespoons sweet butter, softened
²/₃ cup granulated sugar
1 teaspoon grated lemon rind
    (use the already prepared kind
    that comes in a bottle)
3 eggs, well beaten
1 cup water
1 cup flour
1 cup vegetable oil
1 cup confectioners' sugar mixed
    with 1 teaspoon cinnamon

Utensils

measuring cups and spoons
mixing bowl and spoon
frying pan
tablespoon
paper towels
serving platter

HERE'S HOW TO DO IT:

1. In the mixing bowl, combine the butter, granulated sugar, and lemon rind. Add the eggs, mixing thoroughly. Add the water and flour to make a soft dough.

2. Ask an adult to help you turn on the stove and do the cooking. Put the vegetable oil in the frying pan and heat it up. Using the tablespoon, drop the dough carefully into the hot vegetable oil. When the fritters are brown, turn them over to brown the other side, and then put them on the paper towel to drain. Remove from the paper towels and put them on the serving platter. Sprinkle the confectioners' sugar and cinnamon mixture over the fritters. Serve with maple syrup or honey. Makes about two dozen fritters.

Dulce de Leche— Sweet Milk Dessert

Everyone in Argentina knows and loves this wonderful butterscotch-type sauce that is spread on bread like peanut butter, poured over ice cream, used as a filling for butter cookies, or just eaten by the spoonful.

HERE'S WHAT YOU WILL NEED:

Ingredients

1 can of condensed milk
water

Utensils

medium-size saucepan
mixing spoon

HERE'S HOW TO DO IT:

1. Shake the can of condensed milk very well.

2. Place the unopened can in the saucepan and cover it completely with water. Ask an adult to help you turn on the stove and also watch while this is cooking. Boil the water rapidly for 1½ hours, making sure that the can is always covered with water.

3. Allow the can to cool by itself and then open it. That's all there is to it. Now it is ready to enjoy and share with friends. Store leftover sauce in the refrigerator. Makes about 2½ cups.

Argentina Butter Cookies

These great cookies are made even more delicious because they are filled with dulce de leche in the center. Follow the recipe for dulce de leche and then spread it on one cookie. Top with another cookie.

HERE'S WHAT YOU WILL NEED:

Ingredients
3/4 cup sweet butter, softened
1 cup sugar
1 egg
2 egg yolks
1 tablespoon vanilla extract
2 teaspoons grated lemon rind (comes in a bottle), optional
1/2 cup cornstarch
1 1/2 cups flour
1 teaspoon baking powder
extra flour to dust the rolling pin and cutting surface
extra butter to grease the cookie sheet

Utensils
measuring cups and spoons
mixing bowl and spoon
rolling pin
small glass, to cut out cookies
cookie sheet, pot holders

HERE'S HOW TO DO IT:

1. Combine the butter and sugar in the mixing bowl. Stir until completely mixed. Add the egg and egg yolks, beating until light and fluffy. Add the vanilla and lemon rind. Stir in the cornstarch, flour, and baking powder. Mix thoroughly.

2. Ask an adult to help you turn on the oven and bake the cookies. Preheat the oven to 325°.

3. Roll out the dough to ¼" thickness on a clean, lightly floured surface. Cut the dough into rounds with the open side of the glass. Place the cookies on a greased cookie sheet about 1" apart. You will have to use two cookie sheets, or bake them in two batches.

4. Bake for about 20 minutes, or until lightly browned. Set aside to cool. Spread about a tablespoon of dulce de leche on one cookie and top with another. Continue until all of the cookies are used. Makes about eighteen to twenty single cookies.

Caribbean Fruit Punch

Fresh fruit is plentiful and delicious on the islands. This tasty drink is easily made in a blender or food processor.

HERE'S WHAT YOU WILL NEED:

Ingredients
1 small can of crushed pineapple, with the juice
2 cups orange juice
1 cup maraschino cherries
1 banana, peeled and sliced
1 apple, peeled and sliced
½ cup strawberries, with tops removed

Utensils
measuring cups
blender or food processor
six glasses

HERE'S HOW TO DO IT:

1. Combine all of the ingredients in the blender or processor and mix until it becomes a liquid, about 2 minutes. It will be thick and foamy.

2. Pour the drink into glasses. This makes about six servings. You can also try experimenting with different combinations of fruits.

Index